A Pagan's Path to Meditation

10 Meditations for Yoga and Nature Lovers

Val Rogers

Artwork by Linda Tracy

Rogers, Val. *A Pagan's Path to Meditation: 10 Meditations for Yoga and Nature Lovers*

Copyright © 2023 by Valerie Rogers. All rights reserved.

No part of this book may be reproduced in any form or by any electronic or mechanical means, including information storage and retrieval systems, without written permission from the author, except for the use of brief quotations in a book review.

ISBNs: 979-8-9883020-0-1 (paperback)
        979-8-9883020-1-8 (ebook)

Library of Congress Control Number: 2023920550

KWE Publishing, www.kwepub.com

Find out more about "Val's World" at ValRogers.Net

This book is dedicated to time.

Your time.

I believe that this is the right time, the right place, and the right space for you to lean into the words and experiences that await you on these pages. Will you take the time?

FOREWORD

Valerie has a very unique connection with divine source energy. She moves through life as an open channel, curious and playful as she opens herself to new experiences, surprises, and delights. I met Valerie in the late 1990's in the context of academia, but it was during a group past life regression session years later that our spirits meaningfully connected. We sat in lotus position on overstuffed orange and yellow pillows, eager to see what tales our super conscious would tell us on a warm summer night.

Years later, I was looking for what I thought would be a simple voiceover talent for a series of meditations I had written. I contacted Val asking if she did voiceover work, and she confidently answered, "Of course!" A day later, she sent me an audio file of her bringing one of my meditations to life with her soothing and melodic voice, my mind and body relaxed, drawn in by her hypnotic tones. From that day on, I handed her the proverbial pen and said, meditate and write whatever you sense and feel. And complete magic happened.

Valerie has created some of our most innovative meditations for our meditation app company Cloud9 Online. Valerie remains in service to humanity, putting words to the powerful and healing vibrations of spirit and of Mother Gaia. Valerie modeled the way for our other writers. "Don't think, just feel" and she lives her life exactly that way, trusting her intuition that is always there to guide us down our best path.

I'm delighted to see her ministry continue with what will certainly be her first of many books with divinely channeled words that heal the mind, body, and spirit. A Pagans Path to guided meditation holds you by the hand and takes you on a magical journey into the soul, the sacred space where we are one with source and most at home. The Pagans Path will help anyone who reads it to feel the ease and grace of connecting to source through meditation.

Enjoy your journey, namaste!

~ Delanea Davis - author of *Rune Reading Your Life* & CEO of Cloud9 Online
c9ohealth.com

TABLE OF CONTENTS

INTRODUCTION

At the heart of all Pagans is nature. Not just the beauty but the destruction, too. Not just the light and joy but the darkness, too. And not just life but death. Pagans have an innate way to pinpoint balance in a quick and precise manner. It can be a blessing and a curse. Often, people who feel a lot—a lot of energies, for instance—are drawn into the mysteries of a Pagan path. People who sense outside the traditional five senses are creative and logically empathic, and they can also be curious about the Pagan path.

But what does it really mean to be Pagan? As you might guess, there is no one correct answer. I could just as easily ask what it means to be a woman? Or man? Or brother? Or mother? Based on our own paradigms—our own experiences and interactions with the world—our answers would be uniquely ours. Sure, there are broad strokes of understanding that being a woman holds certain characteristics and qualities, just as being a mother does. Whether we know it or not, we all have traces of energies that build our understanding of what being a woman (or man) means to us. A deep resonance is within us that encourages and encompasses all energies. Even though I am a woman, there are traces of male energies within me. Even though I am not a brother, there still are traces of "brother" energies within me. Whether they are dormant or fresh, I still contain energies of what brother means to me.

In my personal practice, I tend to follow, like a mantra, the Wiccan Rede: "An' it Harm None, Do What Ye Will." It is a basic principle for me to stay focused in understanding that my actions, behaviors, habits, and my words can affect those around me. Yet, we are human, with human feelings, so this may be nice on paper, but in practice it can be challenging. For instance, we all know we should be kind to others. That sounds simple and easy. Yet when we are hurt emotionally or physically, it is not so easy to express being kind in the moment. Have you ever been fired from a position you love, or been hurt deeply by the words of someone close to you? Instant reaction is what we express. What that instant reaction looks like can be rooted in fear, or love. Often, we tend to defend ourselves. We can lash out. Being kind to the person who inflicted that pain on you is not an easy mindset to demonstrate. Yet, that is exactly the mastery of the Wiccan Rede: to react instantly with kindness, peace and love no matter what has or is happening to you in the moment.

Humans are the highest level of consciousness on Earth. And being at this high level, we are given gifts every day in every way that allow us to feel the energies around us. We are connected to the "all there is" (and naturally, "the all that is not").

Often, we do not connect with the energies that naturally surround us because we are busy doing human things. Work, family, our beloved pets, and hobbies. Busy, busy, we are. Making and doing busy things.

Muses & Insights

My first semester in college, my English professor taught me a valuable insight that I still carry today. He said, "The word 'thing' can always be replaced with another word. So, mean what you say, and say what you mean. Don't use the word 'thing' as an excuse to be lazy. Find another word to represent that 'thing.'"

One definition of thing is: *"An object that one need not, cannot, or does not wish to give a specific name to."*

"That's just the nature of things."

-On the Nature of Things by Titus Lucretius Carus
(written around 60 BC)

If I chose one word that could describe nature, I would choose the word "balance." To me, nothing exemplifies balance more than nature. It is acutely expressed in all living creatures as well as in the Elements of Water, Earth, Air, and Fire. All living creatures face life and death every day. The lives of many insects, plants, and animals depend upon the very death of others. Nature has been recycling for millions of years. The waste of living plants, insects, and animals provides essential nutrients to other plants, insects, and animals. There could be no life without the opposite—death. Pagans have a deep understanding of this concept.

In investigating nature, life and death are ever-present. Just look at the roadkill, the squashed ant on the ground, or the hunting owl at night. Animals rely on death to live. We humans tend to have it a bit easier. We have learned to create great comforts in our lives to avoid the topic of death and to focus primarily on the "living" aspect of being human. Perhaps if we spent a little more time contemplating and honoring death, we would be able to enjoy life a bit more.

Balance is also seen in the natural Elements that are at the core of Wicca and Pagan practices. Below is each Element and a brief description of its relationship to the cycle of life-death-rebirth.

Water: Water is the relational direction of West. It is a powerful Element that exemplifies the word "clean." Whether coming from the skies, the Earth, or our own bodies, Water purges, cleanses, and refreshes.

Earth: Earth is the relational direction of North. The solidness of the ground. Humans have used the physical Earth to create all material items that have first been manifested in our minds. And yet, rot and decay are needed for new growth to thrive.

Air: Air is the relational direction of East. Stale Air is stagnated and not necessarily easy nor healthy to breathe in. Fresh Air, provided by breezes and wind gusts, whisks away the old dust and debris to provide room for flourishing new growth. It is like nature's vacuum.

Fire: Fire is the relational direction of South. It is the Element of transformation and is considered a cleansing Element to make way for the new. Through heat and purification, newness can arise. Burning is associated with new life, like controlled forest fires make way for new growth.

We cannot live without these Elements. They are ever-present in us and around us. This book contains six meditations related to these four Elements. The first meditation is an introduction to the four Elements. Following are meditations on Water, Earth, Air, and Fire. The last meditation in the Elements series is a conclusion on the four Elements. They can be used individually or in a group practice.

WHY MEDITATION?

Meditation is a fantastic tool that we can use to connect to our inner selves. What this means to me, is that we can utilize meditation to reflect the outer divine and invite it into our inner being. This helps us to create and maintain a balance between the outer world and our inner world. Meditation can be considered a conduit to the soul. It opens doors and passages to the Universal Source. What I find so fascinating about the tool of meditation is that I can tap into it anytime, anywhere, and anyhow. Meditation can be accessible to us every day in every way.

What do I mean by this? Well, meditation does not have to be all ceremonious and formal. We do not have to overthink it. For instance, I can be standing in line at the grocery store and utilize meditation by simply taking a few deep breaths in and out while I wait or calm myself while searching the shelves for my favorite item. This is utilizing the power of meditation. Meditation does not need to be done at a certain time in the day or a certain place. For example, I could be having a conversation with my son that suddenly begins to turn in a negative direction. (Be honest, we all can *feel* this when it begins to happen.) Before I even engage in the energy that I begin to *feel*, I can choose to get behind that energy to let it swell like a wave and then pass. I can do this simply by remaining calm. By taking a deep breath. By reframing my mindset. This is a lot harder to do than we realize. But I encourage you to at least try it. Think about it. The second you begin to *feel* the conversation turning sour, stop. Take a deep breath in and square your body. As you breathe out, relax your muscles. This is meditation in the moment.

Time and time again, meditation has been proven to help relieve anxiety and stress. It has healing powers beyond our comprehension. It can lower blood pressure, decrease physical pain, and improve the functioning of our immune systems, brain, and other important organs in our bodies. For example, the American Psychological Association has found that regular meditation can change your brain and biology in positive ways to improve your mental and physical health. The National Center for Complementary and Integrative Health is a great source of medical grade research studies to point to improved reduction in anxiety, stress, pain, insomnia, weight control and even improved mental health for breast cancer patients and caregivers. *(nih.gov)*

By controlling your attention and relaxing into the calmness of your mind, you are engaging in a positive, helpful activity for your mind, body, and spirit. And while meditation takes discipline, just like working out and eating healthy, it can be practiced anytime, anywhere, in a multitude of styles. There is no such thing as "one way is the right way" when it comes to meditation. In my life, for example, I find that the activities I enjoy doing often put me in a meditative frame of mind. For instance, I love gardening. Gardening to me is not a chore. It is a relaxing, enjoyable activity that I do freely and willingly. I find the time I spend watering, planting, replanting, deadheading, and fussing over the plants and shrubs provides me with the space I need to become centered with nature. It adds value to my life. When I couple my gardening with ten to twenty minutes of eyes-closed, focused breathing, I find the feeling of peace lasts longer throughout my day.

Music is another activity I find great joy in. Whether it's singing, playing, listening, or engaging in musical activities, it provides me with a sense of freedom I rarely find elsewhere. I feel I can soar above the complexities of the day when music is involved. I can get lost in the activity and lose track of time. Before I perform, I often take ten minutes to be by myself and simply breathe. I become centered and focus on being the best I can be right in the moment. This is meditation in the moment.

Many feel this way when participating in the creative side of ourselves, such as dance, art, sculpture, cooking, pottery, or writing. And others find great calmness in physical activity such as swimming, running, walking, archery, biking, horseback riding, and many other sporting activities. Even the activity of driving can be calming for our bodies. Have you ever been driving only to realize you reached your destination without much thought? And as with nature, it is with us, too. A balance. Sometimes, driving can cause us angst and stress beyond measure. Sometimes, my gardening can produce an overwhelming feeling of unproductiveness. Will these weeds ever stop growing? Why did those chipmunks eat my bulbs?

Muses & Insights

Gardening is re-gardening. Just when you think you have it all figured out and it's set to perfection, a rainstorm comes and twists it all around again. And after the storm, I go out once again to pick and pluck and weed and tuck. Oh, the joy and sweat of recreating what I thought I could hold onto.

Can we learn from this and apply the broad strokes and concepts from nature to the complicated-busy living we do? I think we can. And meditation can be a grand tool to aid us in our journey of living and reflection of creating and recreating.

HOW TO USE THIS BOOK

This is not an introductory book meant to explain "What is Paganism?" or "How do you meditate?" Nor is it a coaching book on how to implement nature and pagan practices into your everyday life. There are hundreds, if not thousands, of books and resources on that topic. I need to note here the obvious: While I firmly and deeply believe that meditation can reduce negativity and help us in positive ways physically, mentally and emotionally, I am not a medical professional. You can seek the advice of your doctor to help guide and support you in your mental, emotional and physical health needs. Meditation can be a great tool.

This book includes ten meditations (plus one bonus meditation) specifically designed for the Pagan heart and for those who appreciate nature and seek balance in their lives. Whether you are a yoga guru or an office workaholic, this book is intended to provide you with a freer, cleaner, and greener mindset. I challenge you to take this book and make it your own. Approach each chapter (meditation) with fresh eyes. Take it all in and use your natural creative inspiration to allow yourself to lean into listening to your body, your inner dialogue, and your outer environment. I encourage you to keep an open mind so you may have an honest conversation with yourself.

If you are new to meditation, you might worry about falling asleep. There's no need to. After all, our bodies are most relaxed when we sleep. If the worst thing that happens is you end up taking a nap, then so be it! I encourage you to try each meditation multiple times. If at one point you are nodding off, no problem. Simply enjoy the peace and rest, then try it again another time. One great aspect of meditation is that you can keep on doing it. And the neat aspect about the meditations I have written here is that each time you engage in them, you will find another nugget of truth about yourself. Another piece of yourself may be exposed that you can nurture and mull over. I have specifically included guidance to make the experience different each time you partake in these meditations.

Meditation is not about memorizing the capitals of each state in the United States. It is not a test nor a history lesson. These are private and individualized experiences and exercises so you can delve deeper into your inner truths and desires. Meditation will help you gain insight into who you are and who you choose to be.

There are several ways to allow this book to touch and work with you.

1) **Read the Meditations to Yourself**
   Read the meditations silently to yourself. Find a quiet time that is all yours to claim. All that is needed is about ten to fifteen minutes. Read slowly. You do not need to rush through the passages. There is no conclusion of a story to finish. As you read, allow yourself to breathe in when you read the words. This will naturally aid you to begin relaxing. Open yourself to really think about the words and what they may mean to you. Be inspired by them. All thinking and connecting can be inspiring if we are in the right mindset to receive the messages we hear. Get ahead of yourself and set your intention to be inspired when you read these pages.

2) **Read the Meditation Out Loud**
   Reading out loud takes more outward energy and sets that energy into motion. While you read out loud to yourself, read slowly and carefully. Be thoughtful about your approach. If something does not quite make sense, or you stumble among the words, be inspired to rewrite your own words that resonate with you. Each meditation will guide you and encourage you. At the beginning of the meditation, you are instructed to "close your eyes." Obviously, as you read the meditation you cannot close your eyes, but you can visualize yourself as relaxed with your eyes closed. You can lean into your muscle memory of what it *feels like* to have your eyes closed.

   I often find it pleasing and peaceful to have my earbuds or headphones on with light meditation or spa music playing. This allows my pacing of the reading to be slowed. Read gently without rushing. Try and absorb each word in your own style of contemplation.

3) **Write About the Meditation**
   Using your own words is a powerful, magical exercise. It allows energy to flow from you, through you, and out of you. And then, you can reread and recreate the aspects all over again. A bit like doing the same puzzle again, yet the picture is slightly different the second time you create it.

   Take each meditation individually and begin a journaling book. Be sure to include the date, time, and where you are at the top of the page each time you journal. This way you can look back on your entries and track your stages of being. You can use your journal over time and trace your personal growth. Alternatively, you can use your phone's recording app and begin journaling your thoughts about specific aspects of the meditations that have touched you.

4) **Speak About the Meditations with Others**

If you have like-minded friends, share with them what you are experiencing. Let them be an inspiration to spark a conversation with your tribe. You can simply share your thoughts and experiences with your friends, or you can take it one step further and meet face-to-face with your friends to have a deeper, perhaps more meaningful discussion, about them. Sharing often will open different perspectives that will enhance your life and create positive thought patterns. Alternatively, you can use your phone's recording app and begin journaling your thoughts about specific aspects of the meditations that have touched you. Allow these meditations to add deeper value to your life by sharing.

5) **Record The Meditations in Your Own Voice**

You can use your phone or any other recording device to capture your own voice speaking the meditation. This is a wonderful way to share these meditations in an audible manner. We learn and view the world differently when we isolate one mode of learning over another. Some of us find experiences richer when we are spoken to and engage in conversations. Others find greater joy in quiet visual contemplations, which leads to the next way you can use this book.

6) **Meditate on the Illustrations**

Each meditation is accompanied by a carefully selected illustration. This image is meant to inspire a deeper understanding of the meditation. It is yet another tool you can utilize to enrich your experience. You can also search for or illustrate your own image to accompany the meditations. This is a great way to make the meditation experience uniquely yours.

The images are also available at: ValRogers.Net

7) **Meditation and Yoga**

   Meditation is an important part of traditional yoga practice and can help you reach higher states of relaxation and peace. The meditations in this book are an excellent addition to any yoga exercise. While the practice of yoga helps us to stretch and bring our physical bodies into alignment with the world around us, the meditation practice can encourage our mindset to do the same for our inner world. You can choose to perform the meditation before a yoga session or after. Conducting the meditation before will aid you in clearing the mind to accept the physical gifts that the body needs during the yoga movements. Performing the meditation afterward will encourage the mind to relax deeper. This can be beneficial in opening your entire body and mind to reset the energy levels needed to create long-lasting benefits after the yoga practice is completed.

Each of these meditations has been carefully selected to add value to any yoga practice. They can incorporate poses of your choice and can become an integral component to your daily, weekly, or other regular class routine. For those yoga enthusiasts interested in a deeper dive into meditation, you can incorporate the illustrations into the experience. All the meditations in this book are linked with a specific illustration that enhances the senses when experiencing each meditation. I invite you to explore ValRogers.Net to discover the many images and products available. Among other treasures, you will find full tapestries in many sizes that can be hung near your altar or in your space of practice.

ABOUT THE ILLUSTRATIONS: BEFORE YOU BEGIN

Each meditation is accompanied by an illustration by artist Linda Rondeau Tracy. These are original illustrations done in soft pastels. Pastel paintings are different from watercolor paintings in that watercolors are inherently transparent, and pastels are inherently opaque. Being opaque, I believe, allows for further depth and interpretation for you to create an intimate experience. The illustrations are meant to enhance your meditative experience. These pastel paintings spoke to me as a perfect fit for this book on meditation because of their common theme of nature.

Before each meditation begins, I have provided a few "Muses & Insights" to describe the connection between the illustration and the meditation from my eyes in my moment of experience. These are meant to be used as inspiration. I encourage you to seek your own explanation and create your unique connection to the illustration as it relates to you in your moments.

Each time you read and reread these meditations, you may discover something different. For instance, you may notice something you didn't see before in the illustration that now speaks to you. Or maybe you are inspired to create your own illustration to match your feelings at the moment. Go for it! Create, paint, draw, and color outside of the lines. There is no "one-size-fits-all" to experience the illustrations and meditations.

ABOUT THE MEDITATIONS: BEFORE YOU BEGIN

Before you begin, I recommend the following:

❖ Find a quiet place. Any place where you know you will be undisturbed for at least ten to fifteen minutes. It could be in your car parked in a parking lot. It could be your bedroom or even the bathroom. The truth is, it doesn't matter where you are as long as you feel comfortable and secure. Many people choose to sit in an upright, strong position, either with their legs crossed or sitting in a chair with their feet firmly planted on the ground. Others find lying down relaxing and comfortable.

❖ Set your intention. Setting your intention does not need to be a huge act of fanfare. All you need to do is state either out loud or to yourself, "I will make this time mine." Alternatively, you can set a clearer intention on a question or issue that you are grappling with. Perhaps you wish to have clarity over a work problem or guidance on how to deal with a spouse or one of your children. Set the intention out into the ether and ask for it. It could sound something like, "I am now surrendering to the answers I need to know to help me become clearer on ________." Fill in the blank with your own personal challenge.

❖ Each meditation is in a separate chapter. Each meditation has a carefully selected original nature illustration to accompany the meditation. Use this visual to your advantage to stimulate energy within yourself. Either before or after you read the meditation, really look at the picture. What do you see? What moves you? What disturbs you? How does it make you feel? Use a journal to chronicle your impressions, insights, and feelings. This will help you to build upon your experiences as you keep enhancing your personal growth journey.

❖ Each meditation will begin with the title and a few sentences describing what the meditation is about. This is intended to ground you in the meditation before you begin.

❖ Each meditation has an opening and a closing line, so you will get clear signals when the meditation is beginning and ending.

❖ As you read the meditation, breathe. When you read the words, "Take a deep breath in. And hold it, then release it," actually do it. Do not just pass this part off. This is one of the most important pieces of this book. Meditation is breathing, just as living is breathing. Don't skimp on breathing.

❖ After the meditation, give yourself as much time as you need. There is no need to rush or worry. Everything is always working out for you, so lean into it! Enjoy your experiences and time with yourself. Remain open to hearing the subtle messages your body, mind, and soul are giving you. Be amazed at the strength you have!

Now, let's begin!

MEDITATIONS

CHAPTER ONE

Grounding Meditation

Setting the Intention

This guided meditation will help calm all those thoughts racing through your mind. It is intended to aid you in grounding yourself from the crazy of the day and all that swirls around you. It can be practiced anytime during the day, maybe during your lunch hour while sitting in your car. It can help refresh your mind and spirit, so you can be prepared to be grounded when dealing with the challenges that you face.

Muses & Insights on the Illustration

Grounding, to me, means being connected to oneself and the Earth. It also means to me the ability to be connected to the outer source of life. It is a triad. Myself, my Earth, my outer self. Some might think of it as my body, mind, and spirit. It is all connected by an invisible thread of energy. This illustration, titled "Here Comes the Sun!," demonstrates this triad connection. The trees represent myself, their roots driving deep into the Earth for stability protected by the layer of fresh snow represent the connection to my Earth. And, the strong winter sun piercing through the bare branches represents the connection to the Universal source, your outer self.

Peaceful blessings to you!

Welcome to your grounding meditation.

You have dedicated this moment in time as your sacred time. Your sacred space to feel safe, secure, and loved every day in every way.

The flow of energy that is here is constantly shifting, moving, and changing… within…and without.

This is your time to be grounded in your truth. Your life. Your Earth. Your change.

In a sitting position, with your eyes closed, take three slow deep breaths in— and release them.

Gently, fully, and slowly. And again…and now, once more…

> (pause)

Acknowledge where your feet are right now.

Are they firm and flat on the surface? Are they supported on a surface? Relaxing all your muscles, take another breath in…and release it. You feel safe, free, and relaxed.

Imagine a tree root developing on the bottom of your spine.

This root extends downward from you, through where you are seated, through buildings, through the layers that separate you from the Earth.

Down, down this massive root travels.

Soon, you sense this root touching the Earth. It breaks the crust and reaches far into the Earth until it is at the center.

> (pause)

From the crown of your head, picture tree-like limbs developing outward toward the sky. They are forming at great speed from the chakra at the top of your head.

These limbs grow and reach and stretch toward the sky till they bend and create a complete circle around you.

They are like an umbrella surrounding you. They gently sway…and you feel peaceful and at ease.

Now, imagine at the center of your chest, at your solar plexus chakra, a warm, bright ball of energy.

A fireball that is glowing bright with light and energy. Breathe in… hold it… and breathe out.

It is building up and emanating from every crevice of your being.

The fireball grows intense and brighter still. It shines into every cell in your essence. It is YOU. It is all of what is and what is not.

Instantly, you realize this is the energy of love. Pure love and light.

Relish this warm fireball of energy for a moment. You are safe and feel loved.

Breathing in easily, and breathing out…

    (pause)

Sit with the strength and ease that this fireball of energy gives you. This gift is always inside you.

From your base, you feel solid.

You are connected to the Earth.

You are grounded to this rock we call Earth that is spinning in space.

As you breathe in, feel a sense of peace begin to fill and spread over and into your entire body.

This feeling of peace seeps out of you.

Gently flowing and washing all around you.

Focus on your breathing. In and out.

In and out.

(pause)

The fireball begins to die back ever so gently. It still shimmers brightly, but it is now fading ever so slightly, like the dial on a dimmer switch. And while it may dim, you gain the wisdom that it is always burning inside you.

The fireball is always within you. It is a light that cannot die.

(pause)

Take a breath in…and let it go…

The limbs that have extended outward from your head that wrap around you now begin to retract. They fly effortlessly back to the crown of your head, where they remain as small, tiny stubs.

The root begins to retract back into your spine. Being pulled up, up, up. Now, the root reaches the bottom of your vertebra where it remains.

You are grounded.

You are solid.

You feel at peace.

Begin to wiggle your toes and fingers, gently bringing you back to the present.

Breathing in. Breathing out.

When you awaken fully, you know, without a doubt, that you are connected to this fireball of energy.

You are connected to the Earth.

(pause)

You've just completed an important part of your day. This was your time to feel protected and to claim your power. You are safe. You are life. Well done!

Breathing in. Breathing out.

As you prepare to take on the next steps of your living, remember, you are connected and protected by the light that shines within you and without you. You are the power.

Every day.

In every way.

Peaceful blessings to you

as you go about your way.

CHAPTER TWO

The Power of Your Thoughts

Setting the Intention

Life is busy. We are busy humans doing busy "things." The intention of this meditation is to bring us back to the simple concept that we are what we think about. Since we are often "so busy," our minds rarely get a chance to rest. To chill. To take a break from the noise. This meditation can aid us in resetting our goals. In reforming and reconnecting to what is important to us.

Illustration: Muses & Insights

When thinking about how our thoughts create and interact with our experiences, I often imagine a bubbling stream of Water gently gliding over rocks and sticks. Where does that Water go? Where did it come from? This drawing, to me, embodies the essence of our wandering thoughts. In the background of this illustration, titled "Hop River State Park Trail," you see the solidness of the bridge. This represents the solidness of the Earth we live on. Our guidepost. Our touchstone. While our thoughts can be meandering by us, we are always connected to our bodies and grounded in the "here and now." When we have negative thought patterns, we can get stuck on the rocks, the sticks, all the debris blocking us from flowing. That can compound the challenges we face every day. By releasing these negative thoughts into the flow of the Water, we can begin to ease into a more peaceful, positive mindset. While the rocks and sticks may always be there, so is our choice to flow around them.

Peaceful blessings to you!

Welcome to the power of your thoughts.

You have dedicated this moment in time as your sacred time. Your sacred space to feel safe, secure, and loved every day in every way.

The flow of energy that is here is constantly shifting, moving, and changing… within…and without.

This is your time to connect with the power of your thoughts. Your voice. Your life. Your change.

In a sitting position, with your eyes closed, take a deep breath in and release it.

Feel how it moves inside you as you breathe in again.

The Air is cool.

So free.

So pure.

This is your Air.

Breathe deeply.

It fills you more.

Now, let it go.

(pause)

What you think, you create. It's massive and incredible. Yet, in the same breath, it's minuscule and can be seen as completely insignificant.

But it is always there.

It is all thoughts.

There may be people in your life that influence you. Some may encourage you to share your thoughts with them.

Others may want to tell you exactly what to think. How to think and when to think.

The truth is, only you have control over what you think.

You have the power to harness and train your thoughts and feelings to serve you. In the blink of an eye, you can change a thought…and, rather remarkably, your entire experience shifts.

Breathe in and hold it. What are you thinking now?

And let your breath glide from you.

    (pause)

What you think will be drawn to you. What is your desire?

What is your wish in this moment?

Breathe in and think about that desire…

    (pause)

It can be as big or small as you want.

It can be as outlandish or as common as you think.

    (pause)

It's YOUR desire. In this one "blink" moment of time. No one can take this away from you.

Your desires may shift and change every time you meditate. And this is perfectly fine—since we are always constantly shifting and changing. It only makes sense that as we experience our life, our thoughts and desires also shift and change.

This is not a "one-and-done" desire. It is an evolution of desires that allows us to experience our love and life in a fuller, deeper way.

Relax into your breathing.

In and out.

Again…in and out.

> (pause)

Let it fill your mind.

Let it consume your body.

Let this desire pour into your soul.

Acknowledge this thought. Your thought. Own this desire. Your desire.

Say it again. Inside your mind. As you take another breath in, repeat your desire. Say it to yourself. Let it fill every crevice of your physical body and flood into and out of your center.

> (pause)

You are a remarkable soul experiencing the life you create—your life—in your body. Own your body as perfection for you at this given point in time. You may not see it as perfect, but it is perfectly…
beautifully, and
physically exactly as it needs to be right now.
Your body helps your soul experience the thoughts you create.

It changes.

Thoughts change, bodies change, energy changes.

Experiences change.

The amazing truth is—what you think, you will create. This will be your experience. Do you think you want a different experience than what you are having in your life now?

Then think.

Think it. Desire it.

Change starts with your thoughts. You are the power of your thoughts.

> (pause)

Sit here with this feeling of desire filling your body and every inch of your being for as long as you need.

(pause)

When you are ready, begin to sense around you the day you will return to. You breathe in the smell of the space you are in and stretch your hands, feet, and body. Roll your shoulders and neck.

As you bring yourself back to the present time, know that you've just completed an important part of your day. This was your time to claim your desires. To claim the power of your thoughts. You are safe. You are life.

Breathing in…and out.

As you prepare to take on the next steps of your living, remember that you are connected and protected by the light and desire that shines within you… and without you...you are the power.

Every day.

In every way.

Peaceful blessings to you

as you go about your way.

CHAPTER THREE

Protection Meditation

Setting the Intention

Sometimes, we may feel that we are entering into a situation where others may attack our spirit and wellness. This meditation focuses on our strengthening power which will protect our inner core. It is meant to repel energies that may harm us. This meditation will guide you through a short, relaxing exercise that calms the mind, allowing the spirit to call forth the white light energy that will form a strong, loving barrier around us that will last as long as we desire.

Illustration: Muses & Insights

Imagine yourself coming back from a long, hard journey. You are tired. All you desire is the peacefulness of home. The comforts of your space, friends, and family. When you look at this illustration, which Linda has titled "In Winter," what do you see? A cabin. A snow-covered scene with a tree in the forefront. A sunset? A sunrise? The horizon is curved, resembling the protection of a mother's womb. The forefront of the fence and the tall pine tree that glistens with fresh snow is our guidepost to find home. The place we feel safe. It is cozy, well-lit and welcoming. The added layer of snow protects the Earth below like a warm blanket that is placed around our shoulders after a long journey. The energies represented here are positive, pure, safe, and freeing.

Peaceful blessings to you!

Welcome to your protection meditation.

You have dedicated this moment in time as your sacred time. This is your sacred space to feel safe, secure, and loved every day in every way.

The flow of energy that is here is constantly shifting, moving, and changing… within…and without.

It is your time to create protection from energies that no longer serve you or energies that you sense may be harmful to you. It is your time to feel the comforts once again of safety and security.

In a sitting position, with your eyes closed, take three slow deep breaths in— and release them.

> (pause)

As you take a slow deep breath in…think about what energies and blocks you may be experiencing.

> What is draining you?

> What is attacking you?

> Who is attacking you?

> Hold these thoughts in your mind…

Take a breath in and as you exhale…let those thoughts and energies go—out with your breath…they are yours no longer.

Watch them leave and then slowly dissipate—like the mist—without a sound—into the darkness…into millions of tiny pieces.

They scatter and are absorbed instantly by the darkness.

> (pause)

Breathe in…hold…and breathe out.

In the distance, you sense a candle burning…it is so far away, you almost can't tell that it is a single flame of a tall white candle.

As you breathe in, the flame flickers ever so slightly at the intake of your Air.

With your exhaled breath, it dances higher into the darkness…it pulls you closer to it.

You glide effortlessly toward this flame, the strong, brilliant flame burning at the top.

You pick it up and hold it above your head, noticing the perfect circle of light at your feet…

You breathe in. You breathe out.

Love, warmth, and power fill you. This candle holds great power to protect you. It is love and pure peaceful energy…

    (pause)

You place the candle at your feet in front of you. And as you take a step back, you see a thin wall begin to rise from the circle of light that is created from the candle glow on the ground.

The wall is almost invisible, yet you feel it shimmer with strength and power. It grows tall and wraps around you—high above your head…

You are in a bubble of purity, strength, peace, and love…

You feel safe and strong.

    (pause)

In the distance, you see tiny particles grouping together and moving toward you at great speed. You feel the invisible wall of light pulsing with warm energy.

As the particles zoom toward you, you realize they are the negative energies you have just exhaled. They grow bigger as they attach to each other…yet, amazingly, they cannot reach you.

Your wall of pure white light protects you.

They cannot penetrate your wall. They bounce off and fly away.

You have repelled them so all that fills you is warm, strong, loving energy.

As you take another breath in, claim this power of the light as yours. Sit with this peaceful feeling for a while and know you can come back to this peace as often and as long as you like…

    (pause)

You've just completed an important part of your day. This was your time to feel protected and to claim your power. You are safe. You are life. Well done!

Slowly begin to wiggle your toes and fingers, gently bringing you back to the present.

Breathing in…breathing out.

As you prepare to take on the next steps of your living, remember that you are connected and protected by the light that shines within you and without you. You are the power.

Every day.

In every way.

Peaceful blessings to you

as you go about your way.

CHAPTER FOUR

Bringing Forth Gratitude

<u>*Setting the Intention*</u>

In the busyness of the world we create, staying focused on being grateful for all we have may be the furthest thing from our minds. But, acknowledging and bringing forth the sincere feeling of being grateful is powerful. Taking stock in our blessings shares with the universe our intent to keep these blessings around for us. Our lowest points are the most important times to focus on our wealth of all we have present in our life right now. Join me as we bring forth gratitude.

<u>*Illustration: Muses & Insights*</u>

This illustration, titled appropriately "Poppies," has special meaning to me as my mom and I used to discuss—in depth—the beauty of the petals, the intricacies of the stem, and the hardiness and randomness of where the flowers would magically appear each spring. The red poppy has long been associated with remembrance, hope, peace, and gratitude. In 1920, the red poppy became the official flower of the American Legion family to honor and give thanks to those soldiers who fought and died during World War I. Be inspired by this beautiful, whimsical image to bring forth gratitude and peace in your life today.

Peaceful blessings to you!

Welcome to your meditation on bringing forth gratitude.

You have dedicated this moment in time as your sacred time. Your sacred space to feel safe, secure, and loved every day in every way.

The flow of energy that is here is constantly shifting, moving, and changing… within…and without.

This is your time to be thankful and grateful for all you have in your life right now in this moment of time…today is the day to bring gratitude closer to you.

In a comfortable position, with your eyes closed, take three slow deep breaths in—and release them.

One…
Two…and
Three…

    (pause)

In this perfect space and time, allow yourself to take stock of the massive abundance in your life right now…

If things are difficult for you at this moment, then now it is even more important for you to bring forth your gratitude and acknowledge your blessings.

Think about the big things and the small things…all the things that are present to you.

    (pause)

All these fascinating things that pop into and out of your life. That, literally, are there for you without question—to aid you in creating who you are…and who…you seek to be.

Create a small list in your mind now…as you take a slow, measured breath in…and release it.

Is it hard to come up with a list?

Think clearly and purposefully about everything in your life…you have so much…so much, that sometimes in this hectic world—in our hectic minds—we may take it for granted.

We may not see it. May not sense it. Yet, it is right there in front of you. Listen to your intuition.

What do you hear?

(pause)

As you take another breath in…slow it down…and release it.

Slow your mind down to focus…focus on one word…grateful.

Grateful…let it touch you—for just a few seconds—grateful…

(pause)

As you focus on the word GRATEFUL, I'd like you to select several things you are sincerely thankful for that are in your life right now.

I know, this may be difficult to do—especially if you feel you are not where you wish or think you "should" be. But for right now, place the should'ves, the could'ves, and the would'ves on a shelf.

Give that dialogue a rest. And focus on the joy your heart can feel when you think about being grateful.

Grateful.

Take a deep slow breath in…and release it.

Pull to your mind the first thoughts that come to you, to be grateful about… hold them there in your mind's eye…and complete this sentence in your head:

I am grateful for_______________________

(pause)

Are they big things? Like health, family, paycheck, and home?

Are they small things that we might take for granted…like running Water, shoelaces, coffee, your mother's hand on your face, the ability to caress your pet when you arrive home…?

(pause)

All of it matters. The big and small…choose a few, right now, and say to yourself, "I am grateful for" and fill in the blank.

I am grateful for ____________________

Breathe in…

I am grateful for ____________________

Breathe out…

I am grateful for ____________________

Take another slow, measured breath and bring forth these gifts for a count of ten…

(pause)

One, I am grateful for
Two, I am grateful for
Three, I am grateful for
Four, I am grateful for
Five, I am grateful for

(pause)

Six, I am grateful for
Seven, I am grateful for
Eight, I am grateful for
Nine, I am grateful for…and
Ten, I am grateful for…

Sit here in this space of deep gratitude for as long as you need.

When you are ready, slowly begin to wiggle your toes and fingers, gently bringing you back to the present.

Breathing in. Breathing out.

Stretch as you need to, and hold close to the feeling of thankfulness you have just experienced.

Breathing in. Breathing out.

You've just completed an important part of your day. This was your time to feel relaxed and connected to all the little and big things in your life that are always there for you. You are thankful. You are grateful. You are loved.

As you prepare to take on the next steps of your living, remember that you are connected and protected by the light that shines within you and without you. You know the power of gratitude.

Every day.

In every way.

Peaceful blessings to you

as you go about your way.

CHAPTER FIVE

Elements: Introduction Part 1 of 6

Setting the Intention

Water, Earth, Air, and Fire are the natural Elements that swirl in and out of our lives every day. Learning more about how each Element is present and can affect our body, mind, and spirit is a personal growth journey. Understanding more about the Elements can be helpful in healing and in creating balance in us. This meditation is an introduction to the four Elements and provides a brief overview of each. This introduction can be used separately, to reconnect to the energies of the Elements, or as Part I of 6 of the Elements Meditation Series.

Illustration: Muses & Insights

The image chosen for the introduction to the Four Elements, which is titled "Fog on the Fenton," might bring to your mind the mists and fog of a new day emerging. Or it might bring to mind a long, peaceful day closing. Whether you see a new day or the setting sun, the softness of this drawing blurs the lines. In the center, the focus is the stillness of the Water, allowing the solidness of the trees to be reflected gently on the surface. The Elements of Water, Earth, Air, and Fire all are present, playfully and peacefully merging together as if to say, "Can you find me?"

Peaceful blessings to you!

Welcome to the Four Elements Meditation.

You have dedicated this moment in time as your sacred time. Your sacred space to feel safe, secure, and loved every day in every way.

The flow of energy that is here is constantly shifting, moving, and changing… within…and without.

It is our time to connect to the four natural Elements that are present in your life. Whether you know it or not, you have them all in you right now: Water… Earth… Air…and Fire…all connected to your spirit, mind, and body.

In a comfortable position, with your eyes closed, take three slow deep breaths in—and release them.

(pause)

As you take a slow deep breath in…think about what elemental energies you relate to most…at this moment.

Which one intuitively speaks to you right now?

They are always changing. There is no correct answer.

The answer is what feels right to you…right now.

As you begin to know and get in touch with the elements, you begin to know yourself again.

(pause)

Breathe in and allow yourself to feel connected to the Element that speaks clearest to you. Is it…

Water?

Earth?

Air?

Fire?

Take a breath in…and let it go.

Water: Direction of West. The setting sun. The swirling waves. Your subconscious. Your dreams.

The emotions that reside with you daily.

The colors green, blue, and purple.

The sound of spirit talking to you. Think to yourself about these Water qualities. Do they speak to you now?

I am romantic…
I am a great listener…
I am knowing…
I am sensual…

My friendships are deep and loyal.

Listen gently to Water…do you feel it?

    (pause)

Take a slow breath in…holding it, and now releasing it…

Earth: Direction of North—grounding. Mountains and meadows and endless earthy trails.

The solidness beneath your feet.

The colors of brown, green, and gray. Think to yourself about these Earth qualities. Do they speak to you now?

I enjoy my home…
I am not afraid of hard work…
I have a green thumb…
I keep my promises…
I have the strength to deal with adversity.

Listen gently, Earth…do you feel it?

(pause)

Take a slow breath in…holding it, and now releasing it…

Air: Direction of East— the rising sun. The new beginning. The breeze, wind, and clouds. A bird on the wing.

The colors of yellow, light orange, and white. Think to yourself about these Air qualities. Do they speak to you now?

I enjoy reading…
I am smart…
I am a planner…
I don't lose my head when a crisis occurs.

Air—can you feel it?

(pause)

Take a slow breath in…holding it, and now releasing it…

Fire: Direction of South. Inspiration. Transformation. Movement.

The colors of red, bright orange, and dark pink. Think to yourself about these Fire qualities. Do they speak to you now?

I am passionate…
I am brave…
People are drawn to me…
I am creative.

Gently listen, Fire—do you feel it?

Take a breath in…and let it go.

Did one speak to you a little more than another? Did you recognize yourself in all of them?

Take time now to think about all the Elements and how they interact with each other and with you.

(pause)

Water…Earth…Air…Fire.

Sit here and feel the Elements swirling and moving and speaking to you for as long as you feel comfortable.

(pause)

Each time you come back to this meditation, one Element may speak louder. That's a beautiful aspect of the Elements since they shift and move and change.

When you feel ready, slowly become aware of your surroundings by stretching and wiggling your hands and feet. You are moving into the present now…

Gently breathe in…and out…

(pause)

You've just completed an important part of your day. This was your time to explore the power of the four Elements. You are safe. You are life. Well done!

As you prepare to take on the next steps of your living, remember that you are connected and protected by the light that shines within you and without you. You are the power.

Every day.

In every way.

Peaceful blessings to you

as you go about your way.

CHAPTER SIX

Elements: Water Part 2 of 6

Setting the Intention

Water, Earth, Air, and Fire are the natural Elements that swirl in and out of our lives every day. Learning more about how each Element is present can create a positive effect on our body, mind, and spirit. Understanding the Elements can be helpful in healing and in creating balance within us. This meditation explores the way Water connects us to the attributes of our subconscious awareness and our ability to bring forth intuitive powers.

Illustration: Muses & Insights

This drawing reminds me of the song "Splish, Splash," which is also the title. Just hearing those words brings to mind the Water. This illustration depicts Water in action. The fluid motion of Water represents how our lives flow, move, and change. Water is the one Element, out of all the Elements, that can naturally change its form from solid, liquid, or gas just by being exposed to temperature. Water to me is most recognizable in its liquid state. I love this drawing because it is a close-up of Water in action. It could be an ocean, river, stream, or a glass of Water being shaken. It could also represent our inner state of excitement—with the opposite attribute being that of turbulence. Or, it could be your own bathing Water, as you splish and splash. Often, when we bathe, it is a personal and private activity. One that we can create inner space and freedom with. This image brings to life our dreams, subconscious, and deep feelings. How will Water affect you today?

Peaceful blessings to you!

Welcome to your meditation on the powerful Water.

You have dedicated this moment in time as your sacred time. Your sacred space to feel safe, secure, and loved every day in every way.

The flow of energy that is here is constantly shifting, moving, and changing… within…and without.

It is your time to connect to the natural Water. Direction of West. The setting sun. If possible, sit facing or acknowledge where West is to you right now.

In a comfortable position, with your eyes closed, take three slow deep breaths in—and release them.

(pause)

As you take a slow deep breath in…think about the energy Water brings into your life. Think about how Water is always present and around you and in you.

Did you wash your hands today?

Take a sip of iced Water?

Shovel snow?

Did you listen as a friend talked?

Did you remember your dream from last night?

This is all Water being present in your life.

Journey with me now as we experience the Water.

Take a breath in…and release it.

(pause)

Imagine standing on the dunes, overlooking a massive expanse of the ocean. There are no other people in sight. The ocean spreads in front of you from left to center to right. You are high up on the dunes, which gives you a broad, bird's eye perspective.

You can almost see the curvature of the Earth; your view is so tremendous.

You notice a path in the dunes that will take you down to the shore.

You begin to walk. Going with the flow…not rushed at all.

Breathing in, you taste the Air of the ocean—the saltiness—the dampness—the peacefulness surrounding you. It feels good.

    (pause)

You see gulls circling out in the middle of the ocean Water. You intuitively know what is under the waves even though you cannot see beneath the surface. There is beauty there…there is energy there…there is life there.

You make your way down to the shore. Even though you are barefoot, the walk does not hurt your feet.

It is a cloudy sunset, and the beauty is astonishing. The sky is tinged with gray and purple streaks of colors that reach up from the ocean high into the sky. You sense rain.

You breathe in the Air…so pure, so fresh. You feel free and relaxed walking along the Water line of the ocean. The waves greet the sand with the melodic rhythm only the ocean can predict.

Your sense was correct. You feel a raindrop.

You do not wish to escape the Water; rather, you embrace it. The drops of rain continue into a light drizzle. A fog is ahead…adding more moisture to the Air.

Your head is held high. You are getting wet, but you pay no mind to it. You accept it. It is a part of you.

You feel peaceful. You feel dreamy.

Now, gently breathe in…

And out…

What does Water mean to you?

How does Water affect your life?

(pause)

You think about the large icebergs…they reside on the poles of the Earth. Greenland…Antarctica…

Then you think about the opposite of these large masses…you think about the smallest. Perhaps a Water particle…a Water molecule has three atoms: two of hydrogen and one of oxygen.

Think about that…Water has a piece of the Element of Air in it.

How interesting that an Air Element, oxygen, is a part of Water…Air and Water are connected by a tiny common thread.

Taking a slow breath in and out…you become aware that the Element of Earth also has Water particles at its core…and at its surface. And yes, even the sun has traces of H20. In its vapor form, steam has been observed rising over cool sunspots.

(pause)

Take a slow breath in…hold it for a beat…and then release it.

Have you ever thought about how much Water might be in your body? Think about this now…sixty percent of an adult human body is Water, with the brain and the heart containing the most.

Water is essential to so much of our body functioning for survival… from lubricating our joints…to digesting food…to flushing waste…Water is needed for our physical bodies to thrive.

As you focus on your breath now, release into the experience that the Water is both within you…and outside of you.

You have just felt the presence of Water in all the Elements—however small it may be, you have a deep connection to Water. It resides in and out of you.

In…and out…just like your breath goes…in…and out.

You have walked quite a distance on this beautiful beach, yet you are not tired. You feel refreshed, and your heart is open to the wisdom that the Water whispers to you. It shares with you the secrets of sensual grace and intuitiveness meant just for you in this moment. You accept these whispers as they touch your core. Your center. Your spirit.

Listen quietly.

(pause)

When you are ready, you can acknowledge the gifts you have received from the Water. Hold these gifts close to you today. Perhaps make a solid effort to intake more Water today. Be aware of where Water is present to you today.

Slowly begin to wiggle your toes and fingers, gently bringing you back to the present.

Breathing in...breathing out.

You've just completed an important part of your day. This was your time to explore the power of the Water. You are safe. You are balanced.

As you prepare to take on the next steps of your living, remember that you are connected to the power of Water, both within you and without you.

Every day.

In every way.

Peaceful blessings to you

as you go about your way.

CHAPTER SEVEN

Elements: Earth Part 3 of 6

Setting the Intention

Water, Earth, Air, and Fire are the natural Elements that swirl in and out of our lives every day. Yet, they are always constant. Learning more about how each Element is present in us can create a positive effect on our body, mind, and spirit. Understanding the Elements can be helpful in healing and in creating balance within us. This meditation explores the Element of Earth. Earth energy grounds us in our prosperity, wealth, bodies, and our home lives.

Illustration: Muses & Insights

Everything that has ever been produced and created by humankind has come from Earth. Our Earth is not simply a sphere rotating in space; it contains all the materials necessary to physically create our desires. The Earth has provided us with gifts that we can use to manifest our thoughts. It is inspiring to ponder the endless wonders of what our Earth can and has been able to give us throughout our history.

This illustration titled "Twin Trees" represents Earth in its simplicity. Reaching into the twilight skies of a cool midwinter's scene, these two trees stand tall. Perhaps they are a little weathered by the elements of rain, snow, and wind, but their roots that reach into the dirt of the Earth's crust provide a sanctuary of strength from which they pull energy in order to express who they are to the world outside. This is the power of Earth.

Peaceful blessings to you!

Welcome to your meditation on the powerful Element of Earth.

You have dedicated this moment in time as your sacred time. Your sacred space to feel safe, secure, and loved every day in every way.

The flow of energy that is here is constantly shifting, moving, and changing… within…and without.

This is your time to connect to the natural Element of Earth. Direction of North. If possible, sit facing or acknowledge where North is to you right now.

In a sitting position, with your eyes closed, take three slow deep breaths in— and release them.

(pause)

As you take a deep breath in…think about the energy Earth brings into your life.

Are your feet firmly planted on the ground?

Do they feel solid? Or rocky and unsteady?

Earth energy connects us to our physical surroundings.

Our bodies…

Our homes, gardens, families, and our wealth.

Take a slow, deep breath in through your nose…feel it fill your physical body…hold on to it…

And now, let it out through your mouth.

Become aware of your body and how it feels.

Focus on your flesh…muscles…and bones.

Go ahead and stretch. Roll your shoulders…turn your neck, arch your back…flex your feet and hands. How do you feel?

(pause)

In every wondrous moment of our physical existence, gravity pushes us down to be connected to the Earth.

Journey with me now as we experience the Element of Earth.

Take a breath in…and let it go.

You find yourself walking in a damp, dense, dark, deep forest. It is rich with the smell of Earth. You know and understand this smell. In an intimate and primal sense, you know this smell. It feels familiar and safe.

To your right, you see four deer quietly walking the forest ledge. They are not bothered by you, nor you by them. You sense and feel these forest animals and creatures as a part of you.

As you pick your way through the lush forest floor, you come across a large old tree. This is the largest tree you have ever seen—its bark is rugged. Scarred with decades and centuries of weathered stories. Its base is immense. Touch the bark and feel its worth…its steadiness.

Take a breath in…experience this massive wonder…and let it out.

(pause)

You sit on the ground with your back against the tree. You see its twisting, mighty roots ebb and flow out of the ground all around you.

As you marvel at how deep those roots must be, you become aware of the solidness under and around you. You start to feel more and more like a rock that cannot move. You are at peace with this stillness. It feels relaxing and, in a tranquil, mysterious way, it feels good to sit quietly.

You become richly aware of this tree…you are one with the tree. From this tree, you feel the extension and profound connection of the Earth within you.

Take a breath in…holding onto it for as long as you can before gently letting it go.

You have become Earth…you have melted into the tree.

(pause)

Notice the timelessness. You see before you all the living creatures and gifts of nature speed past you…hundreds of years…thousands of years…they change in the forest.

Yet you, you are unmoved by this passage of time.

(pause)

In a moment not bound to time, a spark of loving, pure light gently shines directly at the top of your head, on your crown chakra…you remain molded into the tree, and yet you can *feel* the strength and amazing beauty of love and energy as it opens up your understanding of your own spirituality. Your own existence to yourself.

Can you feel it?

You are enlightened and free and full of love from this energy washing over your head. The light moves to your brow, your third eye chakra, where you are opened to see all that is surrounding you. Your perception is heightened, and you become keenly aware of what your next steps will be. It is all-knowing and simple. It is energizing yet at the same time completely peaceful and soft.

Can you feel it?

The light now begins to glide down to rest on your neck, your throat chakra. It changes color and swirls from calming white to deep indigo, purple to blue. You are still connected solidly to the massiveness of the tree, and yet, you know you can still speak your truth as you see. This light opens your voice so you can communicate to the world your goals and your desires.

Can you hear your voice? Can you feel the power?

Take a slow breath in now…hold it…hold it…hold it…and now, let it go.

As you release your breath, the light shifts and gently glides down over your shoulders and upper arms and rests at your chest, your heart chakra. The light swirls with beauty and colors you have never experienced or seen before. It settles on a warm, glowing green, pulsing with love and sincerity. You instantly feel appreciation and heartfelt gratitude for all the wealth you have surrounding you in your life…give your truthful thanks now for that which you have.

Do you know it? Can you feel it?

(pause)

When you are ready, you become aware of the light shifting, once again, to move effortlessly down your arms and chest to rest peacefully at the top of your belly button, your solar plexus chakra. Glowing from warm green to friendly yellow, this light lingers loosely around your midsection. It opens your confidence, and you become aware of the next steps you can take so you can make the changes you need to sustain your health, wealth, and mindset.

With the tree supporting you, you are solid in your choices and decisions of transformations.

Can you feel it?

Take a slow measured breath in now…and release it. Ahhh, that feels good…

This feeling stays with you and intensifies intimately as the light glides… smoothly down, down, down, to your lower stomach, back, and hips. You feel awakened and alive. You can practically taste your enjoyment. The glow of purity, in the color orange, pulses sweetly with your connection to all.

If the urge strikes you, feel free to stretch and move now. You stay connected to the tree, yet you are flexible enough to reach, twist, and turn.

You feel amazingly connected and firm.

You realize the light has rested steadily at the base of your spine—radiating a strong, simmering, smoldering red warmth. This warmth reaches deep and runs up through your spine to the top of your head, connecting all of your chakras into one long, strong limb.

You emanate strength and freedom of choice. You are connected to the Earth and all the riches it can create.

Can you feel it?

(pause)

Take a breath in and out…

You remain in your tree-like state for as long as you wish.

(pause)

When you are ready, your heart is open to the wisdom that the Element of Earth whispers to you. It shares with you the secrets of wealth, health, patience, nurturing, steady creation, and being ready to express who you are. It provides you the strength to change into who you wish to be…you accept these whispers as they touch your core. Your center.

What do you hear?

(pause)

Breathing in and breathing out, you listen.

(pause)

Hold these messages and know you can act upon them to create the changes you desire. Rolling your shoulders and shifting your neck, you begin to ease out of the massive beauty of the tree. And even though you are easily able to separate yourself from its stoic base, you are connected to it.

You stand up from where you were sitting at the base of the tree and reach high up over your head. In a funny way, you feel like the tree…connected with your roots, your body, perhaps weathered a bit, yet solid, and your arms and your hands reach up, up, and up. You feel blessed and refreshed.

The four deer you saw earlier now pass you on your left. They are much closer than before, and you can see their breath as they breathe in and out the cooling Air. They turn to look at you, and you can see deep into their eyes the quiet knowing of the solidness of Earth. As they blink, begin to wiggle your toes and fingers, gently bringing you back to the present. Stretch and reach as needed to bring you back to the space you began in.

You've just completed an important part of your day. This was your time to explore the power of the Element of Earth. You are safe. You are balanced. You are solid.

Breathing in…breathing out.

As you prepare to take on the next steps of your living, remember that you are connected to the power of Earth, both within you and without you.

Every day.

In every way.

Peaceful blessings to you

as you go about your way.

CHAPTER EIGHT

Elements: Air Part 4 of 6

Setting the Intention

Water, Earth, Air, and Fire are the natural Elements that swirl in and out of our lives every day. Yet, they are always constant. Learning more about how each Element is present in us can create a positive effect on our body, mind, and spirit. Understanding the Elements can be helpful in healing and in creating balance within us. This meditation explores the Element of Air. Air connects us to the attributes of our knowledge, inspiration, thoughts, and universal intellect.

Illustration: Muses & Insights

Capturing the Element of Air is like holding a thought in your hands. It's there, always. We rarely question whether we can think or not, just like we rarely "think" about breathing. Yet, both thought and Air are available to us. We simply breathe in and out. And thoughts come and go. It's almost magical.

The drawing selected here, titled "Something in the Air," embodies the connection Air has to the rest of the Elements. Air touches Water, Air touches Fire, and Air touches the soft, wet sands of the Earth. As it touches them, it changes them. It blends into the other Elements effortlessly. This image is dominated by the sky, where we see the clouds of thought drifting in the sky mirroring the waves as they roll methodically onto the shore. As you gaze at this illustration, relax into it, and enjoy taking a conscious, thoughtful, breath in, holding it for a count of five, then slowly releasing it. How important is the Element of Air to you?

Peaceful blessings to you!

Welcome to your meditation on the powerful Element of Air.

You have dedicated this moment in time as your sacred time. Your sacred space to feel safe, secure, and loved every day in every way.

The flow of energy that is here is constantly shifting, moving, and changing… within…and without.

This is your time to connect to the natural Element of Air. Direction of East. The rising sun. If possible, sit facing or acknowledge where East is to you right now.

This meditation is best done while lying down, but you can sit as needed. With your eyes closed, take three slow deep breaths in—and release them.

(pause)

As you take a deep breath in…think about the energy Air brings into your life today.

Air is always present. It surrounds you…it is in you.

Do you feel it?

Breathe in your Air now, and hold it…and…now, let it escape you…

Air is energy connected to your thoughts and your ideas, and ultimately, it brings formation to your desires.

Journey with me now as we experience the Element of Air.

Take a slow, deep breath in through your nose…feel the Air fill your passages…mind…lungs…body. Your Air travels in through your nose or mouth and quickly moves past your throat and voice box—past your trachea and into your lungs. Each lung breaks out into tree-like branches, so the Air can touch every cell in your body.

Feel your diaphragm expand with the Air. Place your hand above your stomach, just below your lungs, and feel your hand rise and fall with the inhale and exhale. Let's breathe in for a count of four, hold it for seven, and exhale with a count of eight. Ready?

Breathing in…two, three, four—and hold two, three, four, five, six, seven… and release, two, three, four, five, six, seven, eight… Ahhhhh…Air.

And again…in…and hold it…and out.

(pause)

Your diaphragm is the most important muscle in your body for breathing. Located directly below your lungs, this muscle is responsible for pulling Air into your body like a vacuum. Without conscious thought, your diaphragm automatically contracts and retracts. In a beautiful rhythmic fashion, this muscle sustains our life, our breath.

Let's feel that muscle work now by taking a slow, measured breath in…hold it, and now, let it out slowly.

(pause)

Imagine that you are standing at the bottom of a glorious mountain range. It is a beautiful, warm, early spring morning.

The mountains rise high above you into the clouds and blue sky.

The sun is just peeking over the horizon…it will soon begin its long journey of the day.

At the top of the mountains is a special, sacred place…like no other. A wondrous library. Today, you seek to soak in the inspiration of wisdom you know is there. Today, you know your desire to find clarity will be shown to you.

Identify something in your life right now that you wish to understand better. It can be as small or as big or as nebulous as you wish. It can be as easy or complicated as you think. Whatever it is, think now about something you wish to learn more about…

(pause)

A problem…a challenge, an answer, or even a simple nugget of information you've been curious to learn more about. Think about finding a path, a direction to aid you in finding the answers to what you need. Visualize a small gold star—like a sticker a teacher might apply to a paper… think about this star and pour your desire to find your answers into this small star sticker.

Close your eyes and breathe in. As you exhale, you are instantly transported to the top of the mountain.

You are standing on a cobbled pathway. Your eyes open to a beauty few have ever seen…stone and glass structures extend high into the sky. It is colossal. It is magical.

You see two people, a man and a woman. They are older than you…and both carry a sword at their sides. You instinctively know that the sword is not for fighting, but for the protection of knowledge within each of us.

Their style of dress is long, flowy, canary-yellow and made of soft cloth. The breeze flits and flirts with the cotton cloth, exposing a light blue fabric that blends, bends, and changes back into yellow. It is mesmerizing to watch.

(pause)

Birds flutter and float around them as you approach.

"Come," they whisper. "Be inspired…you are a free thinker here."

Breathe in deeply the fresh, cooling Air in this remarkable place.

They escort you into a beautiful building with glass doors that rise three stories high. You wonder how they open without a sound, but that thought is quickly dismissed as you walk silently with them to see the massive interior. What lies before you is a collection of books on shelves that reach as high as the doors—beautiful colors and textures…old books…new books… clean books…dirty books…books on science, history, art, math, gardening, architecture, technology, travel books, and even pleasure books all rise around you.

Take a breath in and then let it out—the beauty is astonishing.

The floor you are on begins to spin and gently glides you around in a circle. A small crystal pedestal rises before you, and you instinctively place your hand on it for stability. You look up but are not dizzy… as you spin, a beam of light streaks sharply through the skylight from the top…the light remains constant as you twirl around and around…it moves up and down like a spotlight on all the books…spinning. You can feel the energy in this room… you are filled with a deep sense of peace at all of this knowledge housed here. The beam of light pauses on a book high, high up. The spinning slows, and you see the book release from its spot on the shelf and begin to float down, down, down to you. It lands with a soft "whoosh" sound onto the crystal pedestal. You see a small shimming gold star on the cover that magically opens to a page.

Take a breath in and lean into what you are about to uncover…

This is your book of the knowledge you seek to move forward with your desired answer…it whispers gently and easily to you the words you need to hear.

Soak in the knowledge you seek. You are smart…you are lighthearted…you are enlightened…you are loved in this space. You are the Knowing.

    (pause)

When you are ready, when you feel you have your guidance, you close the book. In a sparkling blink, the book flies back toward its resting place, back on the shelf where it came from. You watch it rise, up, up, up with the beam of light guiding its way. When you look back down at the crystal pedestal, a sword is now resting there. This is the sword of action. As you pick up the handle, you know knowledge is only as good as the action you take to use it.

Your guides appear on each side of you, and one lifts the sword high into the Air—the beam of light blazes a small golden star into the handle, and your guide hands it to you. This is your sword to carry now.

As they escort you back out into the fresh mountain Air, the other guide whispers to you, "Will you act upon the knowledge you have gained?"

They leave you to sit quietly here on the mountainside with the fresh breeze that whisks at your face. As you breathe in deeply, you contemplate this space and the Element of Air.

You realize that the Air in this massive, mystical mountain library is the same Air you breathe every day. It is hard to determine where Air is divided and separate as it moves so freely.

It is the same Air you breathe in your kitchen. The same Air you breathe when you walk on the ground…the same Air you breathe when you smile at a stranger.

You cannot distinguish when one Air starts and one ends. It simply takes on different aromas, temperatures, tastes…but the Air is one.

Your heart is open to the wisdom that the Element of Air brings to you. It shares with you all the beauty and knowledge of the universe. You absorb this knowledge through every pore of your essence.

Deep into your core.

Can you feel it?

(pause)

Breathing in and breathing out, you listen.

You absorb.

You learn.

Stay as long as you wish in this realm of beauty and knowledge. When you are ready, take your sword in your hand and feel the energy pulse. This sword is etched in your heart, and the gold star shines bright.

Knowledge and action are your goals today.

Slowly begin to wiggle your toes and fingers, gently bringing you back to the present. Stretch and roll your neck and shoulders.

Breathing in…holding…and breathing out.

You are now back to solid ground. Solid space.

(pause)

You've just completed an important part of your day. This was your time to explore the power of the Element of Air. You are safe. You are balanced. You feel refreshed and are armed with the knowledge to take action.

As you prepare to take on the next steps of your living, remember that you are connected and protected by the light that shines within you and without you. You are knowledgeable, and you can choose to take action when needed. You are smart.

Every day.

In every way.

Peaceful blessings to you

as you go about your way.

CHAPTER NINE

Elements: Fire Part 5 of 6

Setting the Intention

Water, Fire, Air, and Earth are the natural Elements that swirl in and out of our lives every day. Learning more about how each Element is present in us can create a positive effect on our body, mind, and spirit. Understanding the Elements can be helpful in healing and in creating balance within us. This meditation explores the Element of Fire. Fire transforms our old energies into new and different energies. It creates a new spark, allowing passion, and creativity to thrive in our lives.

Illustration: Muses & Insights

Although perhaps it is subtle, Fire and ice are evident in this beautiful illustration titled "Snow Sunrise." When you think of Fire, you might think of a campfire, larger bonfire, or even a romantic fireplace slowly burning logs. I chose to stay away from the traditional "log Fire" to express the Element of Fire. Rather, I chose this stunning drawing to express the raw Element of Fire as the sun. I sometimes forget that this massive globe of gas is truly a Fire star. A star so much like the ones I see as I turn my head and heart toward the dark night sky. When I view the stars at night, it is often difficult to imagine the intensity of heat and light that emanates from them as Fire. Yet, Fire it is. Hot and dangerous. Transforming and passionate, Fire can be considered the spark of life. Do you feel it?

Peaceful blessings to you!

Welcome to your meditation on the powerful Element of Fire.

You have dedicated this moment in time as your sacred time. Your sacred space to feel safe, secure, and loved every day in every way.

The flow of energy that is here is constantly shifting, moving, and changing… within…and without.

This is your time to connect to the natural Element of Fire. Direction of South. If possible, sit facing or acknowledge where South is to you right now.

In a sitting position, with your eyes closed, take three slow deep breaths in— and release them.

(pause)

As you take a deep breath in…think about the energy Fire brings into your life. What gives you passion? What drives you to succeed?

We all have an ember burning within us. Sometimes, that ember is very low, and at other times, it is burning high and bright. As you take a slow, deep breath in…think about your ember…

And release your breath.

Does your Air add "fuel to your Fire"? Do you feel it?

(pause)

The Fire Element calls forth desires, passion, and action. It can be exciting and powerful. But if left untamed, it can burn out of control.

Journey with me now as we experience the Element of Fire.

Take a deep breath in…let it reside in your lungs and body…let it burn there… and now, gently push it out.

Let's do it again.

Inhale, one, two, three, four, and hold it for a count of seven, six, five, four, three, two, one, and release it slowly for eight, seven, six, five, four, three, two, and one.

(pause)

Imagine you are high on a rolling hill in front of a large unlit bonfire. You see your loved ones beginning to arrive. It is late summer, and soon, the Air will feel cooler and the nights will appear more quickly. For now, there is a lingering twilight that is refreshing and free.

The logs and twigs are piled high above your head in a perfect circle. There is a sense of excitement in the Air.

You look at the bonfire and think, *It's just wood.* It's just sitting there, doing nothing.

How do you create a spark that can light this Fire? There must be agitation, movement, action to breathe life to create the Fire. Something must be stimulated to start the Fire.

There must be a will and desire to begin.

As you contemplate starting this Fire, a friend invites you to join in at the table they have set up with a variety of food. There is food from the recent harvest of potatoes, corn, carrots, and green beans…there is meat and nuts, fruits and vegetables, and beautiful dishes full of warm casseroles that the smell has your stomach growling. You realize you haven't eaten in a while, and all this food is causing you to be hungry. You need to fuel your body.

Take a breath in and inhale the scents of the Air around you. And let your breath out.

You have eaten your fill and have engaged in hot-topic conversations with friends, family and loved ones. Now, you quietly walk back toward the unlit bonfire.

You close your eyes and call forth your will and drive. Deep within you, you feel it glow and grow. You feel your body getting warm. You feel a tingling sensation. It grows hotter…as you feel it, you realize you have the spark within you to light this Fire.

When you open your eyes, the Fire is lit…surrounding you are your friends and loved ones…a party commences with laughter, tales, stories, and more heated conversations.

Take a breath in…watch this Fire climb and build…and release your breath.

>(pause)

Gaze and get lost in the beauty of the Fire…notice how the flames twist and turn…it creates and destroys at the same time.

Fire is an amazing energy. It transforms darkness into light…provides warmth when there is bitterness and cold. It provides heat for food to be consumed.

Unlike the other natural Elements of Water, Earth, and Air, Fire struggles in a natural state. Its physical form must consume another Element to thrive. It depends on the others. Water tames Fire, Earth can smother it…and Air can feed it.

Be present with your bonfire and loved ones for as long as you wish. Your heart is open to the wisdom that the Element of Fire whispers to you. It shares with you the secrets of sexual freedom and passionate will. You accept these whispers as they touch your core. Your center.

>(pause)

Breathing in and breathing out, you listen.

As you take a slow, deep breath in…think about the energy that Fire brings into your life. Think about how Fire is always present and around you—and in you.

How can the Element of Fire assist you in your life right now?

What does Fire say to you?

What are you passionate about?

What do you need to take action on?

>(pause)

Taking a breath in, holding it, and letting it release from your body, you understand deeply now that the four stages of Fire are represented in your life right now. The stages are ignition, growth, fully peaked, and smoldering decay. Yet, with decay comes new transformation, and new passions arise from the ashes.

This is the cycle of Fire. And so it is true with your passions—your Fire. There is always an ignition, a start, an impetus that gets something moving. Then, it begins to grow and intensify—what a feeling that brings! It crests to a culmination of growth and full development…then it ebbs away to glowing embers only to be brought to life again with new fuel, new desires that change and grow and weave and flow. The cycle.

Sit here for as long as you wish to enjoy the cycle of your Fire.

(Pause)

When you are ready, you watch your Fire dim as it is then fully extinguished. You know that a Fire left untamed can and will burn out of control. Taking a breath in and out, you rise from the bonfire and begin to stretch. Slowly begin to wiggle your toes and fingers, gently bringing you back to the present.

Breathing in. Breathing out.

You've just completed an important part of your day. This was your time to explore the power of the Element of Fire. You are safe. You are balanced. You feel in complete control of your desires.

As you prepare to take on the next steps of your living, remember the spark of creating your desire starts with you.

Every day.

In every way.

Peaceful blessings to you

as you go about your way.

CHAPTER TEN

Elements: Conclusion Part 6 of 6

Setting the Intention

Water, Earth, Air, and Fire are the natural Elements that swirl in and out of our lives every day. Learning more about how each Element is present can affect our body, mind, and spirit. Understanding more about the Elements can be helpful in healing and in creating balance in us. This meditation is the concluding segment of the four Elements. It provides a brief review of each Element. This conclusion meditation can be used separately, to reconnect to the energies of the Elements, or as Part 6 of 6 in the Elements Meditation Series.

Illustration: Muses & Insights

It was important to me to select one of Linda's pastel images that felt different from the others when concluding the Elements Meditation Series. This illustration titled "Peeking Through" displays all four Elements working together. Here you see a stalwart tree with branches reaching and twisting alongside an oceanfront or lakefront. It observes, like a watchtower guard, the horizon of the new sun dawning. The waters, representing the direction of the West, indicate some turbulence perhaps caused by the wind, the Element of Air. The waves of the Water allow the visual of the sun (Fire) to be carried along the tips to quietly rest on the secured shoreline that is the Earth. The ebb and flow of the tide caresses the body of our Earth as easily as the wind may blow and as trustworthy as the sun rises and sets.

Peaceful blessings to you!

Welcome to the conclusion of the Four Elements Meditation.

You have dedicated this moment in time as your sacred time. Your sacred space to feel safe, secure, and loved every day in every way.

The flow of energy that is here is constantly shifting, moving, and changing… within…and without.

This is your time to review and renew the energies of Water, Earth, Air, and Fire. These are the four natural Elements that are present in your life right now. The fifth Element is Spirit. I like to think of Spirit as the glue—and grace—that holds it all together. As above, so below.

In a sitting position, with your eyes closed, take three slow deep breaths in— and release them.

(pause)

Take a deep slow breath in through your nose…let it fill your body…now, release it.

Our elemental energies can be positive, negative, and often a bit in between… they flux and flow…they can be enhanced or agitated by the energies of others. Knowing this can help create balance.

Balance is nature's way.

Our natural tendencies.

As you listen to each Element described…I encourage you to feel.

What snaps and clicks for you right at this very moment?

Remember, these energies change—there is no right or wrong feeling.

While one or two Elements may speak louder to you now, that does not mean to ignore the other two that may have softer voices.

Balance your truths…your Elements.

Take a breath in…and let it go.

Each of us has a Sun sign from the zodiac that we were born under. There are many other energies that make up your zodiac birth chart, and the Sun sign is the most popular—and some even say the most dominant. Do you know your Sun sign? Let's explore them together now.

(pause)

First, we touch upon the Water, the direction of West.

Water is…Feeling.

Romance comes naturally…secret passions are fulfilled…giving is easy.

Secrets can be made and kept.

A walk near the shoreline… the pull of the tides…emotions, feelings, and dreams swim deep in the waters. Both dark and light are the undercurrents of Water.

Take a breath in now, and allow them to wash over you.

(pause)

Those born under the zodiac Sun signs of Pisces, Cancer, and Scorpio are Water signs.

Even though you may not be born under this sign, the Water plays a part in each of us.

The chakra associated with Water is the sacral chakra, located in your pelvis region. Pleasure, creativity, emotions, the dreamworld, sexuality, and fluidity all represent the power of Water.

If you feel emotional, uninspired or stuck, tap into the energies of Water to feel refreshed

with a renewed outlook.

Breathing in… and out.

(pause)

Now, we turn to the powers of the Earth…North.

Earth is…being.

Solid ground. Home is my sanctuary…promises are kept…commitment is met.

The tree of life in the forest.

Deep roots, a strong base, reaching branches…all connected…to Earth.

Take a breath in now—smell in your mind's eye the essence of Earth and walk its sturdy path.

> (pause)

Those born under the zodiac Sun signs of Capricorn, Taurus, and Virgo are Earth signs.

Even though you may not be born under this sign, the Element of Earth plays a part in each of us.

The chakra associated with the Element of Earth is the root chakra, located at the base of your spine. Our wealth, treasures, and the foundation which we build our lives upon all represent the power of Earth.

Feel the stability of Earth under your feet now as you breathe easily in… holding your breath…and releasing it.

Now, let's turn to the Element of Air. Direction of the East and rising sun.

Air is…thinking.

It is intellect.

Knowledge and schooling.

It is researching answers and seeking honesty and authenticity that aids us in understanding the world around us…Being transparent and true to oneself is paramount in the Air energies.

Take a breath in now—and imagine the smell of a new book…you are now being open to new ideas…new thoughts can be created out of "thin Air."

> (pause)

Those born under the zodiac Sun signs of Aquarius, Gemini, and Libra are Air signs.

Even though you may not be born under this sign, the Element of Air plays a vital role in igniting our passions into action.

The chakra that represents the Element of Air is the heart chakra, located at the center of your chest. It oversees our lungs, heart, circulation, skin, arms, and the upper back. I sometimes think the throat chakra also incorporates strong Air Elements, as Air is about clear communication and speaking your mind in an intelligent manner.

(pause)

Thinking outside the box, studying and understanding the way of the world, being "thought-provoking," and clearly communicating with others are all characteristics that represent the power of Air.

Take a breath now, and the Element of Air fill you…and let it out.

Now, we explore the Element of Fire, direction of South.

Where Water is feeling…Earth is being…and Air is thinking…

Fire is…doing.

Passion. Transformation…creating…goal-setting…being a leader and being sure of your desires.

It is a spark. It is smoke. It is an ember. It is a flame. It is ash…all making dreams and deep desires come true with Fire.

Take a breath in…and let it go…

Those born under the zodiac Sun signs of Sagittarius, Aries, and Leo are Fire signs.

Even though you may not be born under this sign, the Element of Fire is still present in us in the form of our deep, burning desires.

The solar plexus chakra, located just above your belly button, is often associated with the Element of Fire. Here our power and self-confidence reside.

Take a slow, measured deep breath in…hold it—let it fill your body…and now, release it out.

Allow the feeling of our desires to rise from within you and spread throughout you…recognize that you have drive, passion, and goals.

(pause)

The balance of the Elements is always swirling within us and without us.

Earth represents our food, which we can only go without for a few weeks.

Water is what we need to drink to live. We can only go without Water for a few days.

Air is what we breathe to live. We can only go without Air for a few minutes.

And what of Fire? The strange Element of Fire? How long can we live without Fire? Not the physical aspect of Fire, but the Fire within us. The Fire that represents our free will, our intentions, passions, and desires. Your soul Fire. How long can you live without it?

Sit quietly for a few moments and think about these Four Elements.

Breathing in and breathing out.

Keep an open mind to what sparks in you.

Balance your truths…your Elements.

Water.
Earth.
Air.
Fire.

Threads. Connections. Circles. Compassion.

Thoughts, ideas, mindset.

Fancies, feelings, freedom.

Action, movement, transformation.

(pause)

When you are ready, slowly begin to wiggle your toes and fingers, gently bringing you back to the present space and time. Stretch your legs and body as needed to feel good.

You've just completed an important part of your day. This was your time to explore the power of the Four Elements: Water, Air, Earth, and Fire. The fifth Element is you. The soul and spirit. You are the glue and grace. You are safe. You are balanced. Well done!

Breathing in...and breathing out...

As you prepare to take on the next steps of your living, remember that you are connected to the energies of the four Elements.

Every day.

In every way.

Peaceful blessings to you

as you go about your way.

BONUS MEDITATION

Connection to the Egyptian Goddess, Isis

Setting the Intention

This meditation calls forth the energies of the great Egyptian goddess, Isis. I have always been drawn to the influence and history of Ancient Egypt. The goddess Isis represents to me the balance of masculine and the feminine. She is strong, cunning, and willing to fight for those she loves. And yet, she is soft, gentle, and tender in her caring for those she loves. When my boys were small, I sang a lullaby to them. It was inspired by my readings and work with Isis's goddess power. This mediation contains the lullaby I sang. The mysteries and enchantment of Isis the goddess reach every corner of the globe and beyond. Her power is your power. Take a few moments now to connect with her to be inspired by her strength and resilience.

Illustration: Muses & Insights

Many images of the great Egyptian goddess, Isis, can be found on the internet. She embodies many symbols, such as the throne, the moon, and her ornate headdress. Yet, it is her outspread wings that are the telltale sign you have encountered her majestic essence. You will find her standing, kneeling, flying, and dancing. Here, the illustration, titled "The Goddess Isis," with its simple, single feather, represents this powerful goddess floating and drifting purposefully toward the light of truth and love. She is gentle and kind, and her wings symbolize protection for all who seek safety.

Peaceful blessings to you!

Welcome to the meditation on exploring the Ancient Egyptian goddess, Isis.

You have dedicated this moment in time as your sacred time. Your sacred space to feel safe, secure, and loved every day in every way.

The flow of energy that is here is constantly shifting, moving, and changing… within…and without.

This is your time to connect with the power that encourages the energies of the Goddess Isis.

In a sitting position, with your eyes closed, take three slow deep breaths in— and release them.

(pause)

Isis is a mighty goddess. She is one of the most powerful goddesses in Egypt. Her reign stretches to all corners of the Earth. Her ancient energy is still alive today.

You can reach it. Feel it and use it to serve you, to honor your path.

Relax your shoulders and chest. Feel your muscles melt into one another.

Your chest melts into your stomach…then into your hips and thighs.

Your mind is clear and relaxed. Your arms, hands, and fingers are soft and light. Your legs are cushioned and comfortable.

Breathing in once more, you melt further into a relaxed position…now, breathe out.

Isis is a healer.

A lover.

A mother.

A warrior.

A goddess.

A goddess of a thousand names. A universal goddess who has endured centuries of incarnations.

Breathe deeply, and bring into your mind's eye your version of the Goddess Isis. Call forth her power to be present with you now.

(pause)

As she joins you in this space right now, feel her loving, mothering power. She is life. She is death, and she is rebirth. All the cycles of creation.

Feel her stories of strength and resilience pour into your mind. Relationships and family are her gifts to you today.

Take a deep breath in…hold it…and let it go.

Think about the relationships in your life right now.

Is there one particular relationship that is feeling a little off track?

Is there one you wish to bring closer to your heart? To love a little deeper?

Call upon the goddess Isis now to guide you and inspire you to persevere in connecting to this person.

(pause)

Let her message wash over you in clear guidance.

Her direction is straightforward. She does not waver on this topic. You are open and able to hear her message.

As you receive your message from the great goddess, feel protected and safe.

Breathing in…and breathing out.

(pause)

Her lullaby brings you strength and peace. Listen now to the words she sings to you:

> May the arms of Isis enfold you,
> Safe may she always hold you,
>
> Near or far, the great mother will hear your call
> Isis is in us all.

The sparkling stars are spinning,
Listen, and you'll hear them singing.

May your dreams be of wondrous things.
Now, sleep gently within her wings.

(pause)

You are connected to the great goddess. She hears your call.

(pause)

You've just completed an important part of your day. This was your time to connect to the ancient power of the goddess Isis. You are safe. You are balanced. You are loved.

When you are ready, slowly begin to wiggle your toes and fingers, gently bringing you back to the present.

Breathing in...and breathing out.

As you prepare to take on the next steps of your living, remember that you are connected and protected by the light that shines within you and without you. You are the power.

Every day.

In every way.

Peaceful blessings to you

as you go about your way.

CONCLUSION

As you experience the world around you, new thought patterns are created in your brain and expressed through you. Change happens in nanoseconds whether you know it or not. Through meditation, we can begin to embrace these changes. Recognize these shifts and changes as pure energy. This is your spiritual growth.

Spiritual growth takes hard work. It is inner work. It is being authentic and honest with the most important being in your world—you. It is hard work because it takes vulnerability, humility, honesty, intention, desire, willpower, strength, and self-reflection. All of this can be painful. And really, who wants to be hurt? However, in truth, identifying our current traits and patterns allows us to catch glimpses of who we are in this moment. Doing this without judgment is the hard part. And once we begin recognizing our behaviors and traits, we can easily change them into creating a different experience. If it serves us, we will change.

Going through pain to reach the side of ease is hard work. Meditation is one tool to aid us in creating who we want to be. Every day, every moment, we have the perfect opportunity to reset our intention and create the grandest version of who we desire to be. The spiritual author, Neale Donald Walsh, wrote in his book *Conversations with God*:

> "Right now, you have the opportunity to create the grandest version of the greatest vision you hold of yourself."

I have personally used this mantra to help me release negative energy and unpleasant vibes I experience in myself.

The Greek philosopher, Socrates, is credited with teaching Athens' youth the following:

> ***"To know thyself is the beginning of wisdom."***

Now, 2,500 years later, we are still wrestling with the concepts and importance of "know thyself." Perhaps it will be a question that never can truly have an answer because it is circular. The more we begin to know ourselves, the more we can recreate who we want to be. So, in turn, we learn. We create. We recreate. It is an ebb. A push and a pull. A flow of Water down a stream, finding its way around rocks and mud and sticks. It is a shovel of dirt being separated and spread. As it falls, it creates its own unique path toward the ground, where once more, it will merge with the Earth in its own pattern. It is a gentle gust of Air that effortlessly picks up the leaf precariously teetering on the branch before it makes its journey through space to land peacefully somewhere it never dreamed it could reach. It is the burning log on the Fire. Through smoke and flame, it shifts and changes to become something else.

Perhaps it is simply a rite of passage for each of us, independently, and quietly to ask the question, "who am I?" Meditation can help us still and quiet the chatter of our inner voice so we can hear the words of our soul. It opens us up to feel, to express, to explore. It will be patient. It will not overtalk. It lies waiting to be heard. My desire through this book is that you have found a space that inspires you to explore the delicate balance of life. That you have an open heart and clear mind to hear the whispers of your soul pointing you toward the answers you desire when you ask, "Who am I?"

ABOUT THE AUTHOR

Val Rogers began her journey of spiritual truth in 1995 after the passing of her mother from breast cancer. Her mother, Joan, was fifty-five years old. At that time, Val was recently married to her high school sweetheart, Scot, and was twenty-four years old. At a complete loss of understanding of why her mom passed and what happens to us when we die, she began her serious quest for spiritual knowledge. She read anything and everything she could get her hands on while exploring and participating in all avenues of religion, personal growth, self-help, women's groups, and spiritual quests.

In 1996, her friend, Barb Nangle, gifted her Neal Donald Walsh's Book *Conversations with God*. His books continue to serve her today as a grounding rod and guidepost to inner growth. She is a constant student—and teacher—of personal growth and spiritual awareness topics and issues. She is particularly drawn to nature and the natural cycle of all living entities. She is a firm believer in the triad of the spirit, mind, and body and uses meditation to balance everyday challenges and demands. She has written and recorded over seventy original meditations for the MediMind Meditation App, which is available at the App Store on all Android and iPhones.

Born under the Aquarian Zodiac Sun Sign, Val embodies the characteristics of the Air sign: creative, energetic, fun, positive, crafty, poised, and innovative. She confidently expresses the introvert and extrovert personality traits and considers herself a balanced blend of a "left-brained" and"right-brained" thinker-feeler.

An accomplished vocalist, writer, arranger, and entertainer, Val has performed for tens of thousands of troops as an esteemed member of the USO for the United States Department of Defense. She continues to perform regularly throughout New England for our veterans as well as for non-profits and at private and public events. She has a deep appreciation for spending time performing in assisted living, veteran centers, and senior centers across the state of Connecticut. She owns Val Rogers Entertainment, LLC. and co-owns the band Red Satin, a high-energy twelve-piece band based in central Connecticut.

Valerie holds a B.S. in communications and a Master of Public Administration (MPA) degree from the University of Connecticut. Her professional career expanded over three decades working first in an environmental non-profit and then later in higher education administration. She has now embraced her destiny to create the life she wants where music, nature, and the health-wealth mindset meet.

Val lives in Northeastern Connecticut and is a proud mother of two young men, Quin (United States Marine Corp) and Cole (esteemed athlete). She resides on her family farm property with her high-school sweetheart husband, Scot, their many chickens, two rescue dogs, two rescue donkeys, hundreds of Christmas trees, and countless weeds in her beautiful gardens.

Find out more about "Val's World" at ValRogers.Net

ABOUT THE ILLUSTRATOR

Linda Rondeau Tracy is originally from Willimantic, CT. She earned a B.S. in music education with a concentration in voice from the University of Connecticut and an M.S. in music education from Central Connecticut State University. She is a retired music teacher, having taught choral music in eastern Connecticut in the Tolland and Windham public school systems for thirty-four years. She was also very active as musical director and choral director for several years for the Windham Theatre Guild in Willimantic, CT. She is the creator and artistic director of the a cappella ensemble, *Take Note!*, based in Mansfield Center, CT, which was formed in 2003. The ensemble focuses on community outreach and has raised hundreds of thousands of dollars, performing benefit concerts throughout eastern Connecticut and beyond, for those in need.

Linda began exploring the world of painting around 2013, when she took an acrylic painting class at her local community center. During one of the painting sessions, the teacher had the class experiment with soft pastels, and Linda was hooked! She liked having direct contact with the paint in stick form and having her hand be the brush. It seemed to create a more personal connection with the art. From then on, she began her journey as a pastel artist, seeking out lessons via the internet and latching onto the teachings of accomplished pastel artists. She has been able to devote more time to this passion upon her retirement from teaching in 2018.

Linda lives in Storrs, CT, where she and her husband, Kevin, raised their two boys, Connor and Brandon.

"Val Rogers has created a collection of meditations for the beginner and adept. Through colorful imagery, she takes us into the heart of the earth's elements. The artwork reflects the beauty and energy of each meditation offering "the beauty way", where we delve into our relationship with the earth, her elements all leading to self-transformation, deeper personal insights for everyday living, and most of all strengthening our interconnectedness to this beautiful planet. This worthy collection enhances our daily practices and is one that will be used often."

~ Judith Dreyer, MS, author of *Navigating Your Dream World*
judithdreyer.com

"If you have been hesitant to give meditation a try, do yourself a favor and read this book. Val's ability to de-mystify meditation makes it approachable and accessible to everyone. Her step-by-step approach to settling into the subtle body is brilliant … how she blends the four elements, goddess magic and beautiful art with her guided meditations is an extraordinary way to guide the mind toward stillness."

~ Sara Daves – author of *Manifest Like a Goddess*
saradaves.com

"Linda Tracy's paintings perfectly complement the meditation practices in this book, evoking qualities of peace, serenity, and oneness. Each work was carefully chosen and skillfully woven into the fabric of the meditation it accompanies with an interpretation by the author. Ms. Tracy's art makes you FEEL what you see by opening your heart and mind to the realm of the possible."

~ Cheryl Chase - Meditation practitioner and art enthusiast

"The pastels of Linda Tracy chosen by author Val Rogers to accompany A Pagan's Path to Meditation have a dream-like quality that invite the viewer to step into the painting, feel the mist, bathe in the tranquility, muse and explore the many paths of beauty available to the meditator."

~ Dr. Dara Blackstone, Music Professor & Conductor

"A longtime admirer of Linda Rondeau Tracy's art, I was moved to see it married with Val Rogers' beautiful guided meditations. To be asked to focus on, for example, a snow-covered cabin in Linda's artistry is hardly a challenge. It's a joy to imagine the warmth and welcome she'd conjure inside. Or the adventure of a bubbling stream. Or the downy protection of a feather."

~ Sue Leroux, Meditator, Writer

www.ingramcontent.com/pod-product-compliance
Lightning Source LLC
Chambersburg PA
CBHW040739120726

48007CB00008B/134